Fugue in G minor
(The Little)

Johann Sebastian Bach

Arranged by Caleb Hudson

THE CANADIAN
BRASS

The Canadian Brass Ensemble Series
Intermediate Level

ISBN 978-1-4950-6306-0

EXCLUSIVELY DISTRIBUTED BY

HAL•LEONARD®
CORPORATION

7777 W. BLUEMOUND RD. P.O. BOX 13819 MILWAUKEE, WI 53213

Copyright © 2016 by HAL LEONARD CORPORATION
International Copyright Secured   All Rights Reserved

For all works contained herein:
Unauthorized copying, arranging, adapting, recording, Internet posting, public performance,
or other distribution of the printed music in this publication is an infringement of copyright.
Infringers are liable under the law.

www.canadianbrass.com
www.halleonard.com

FUGUE IN G MINOR
(The Little)

Johann Sebastian Bach
Arranged by Caleb Hudson

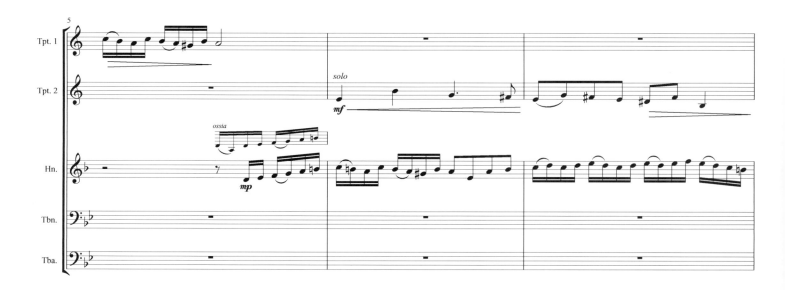

© 2016 Canadian Brass Publications
All Rights Reserved. International Copyright Secured.

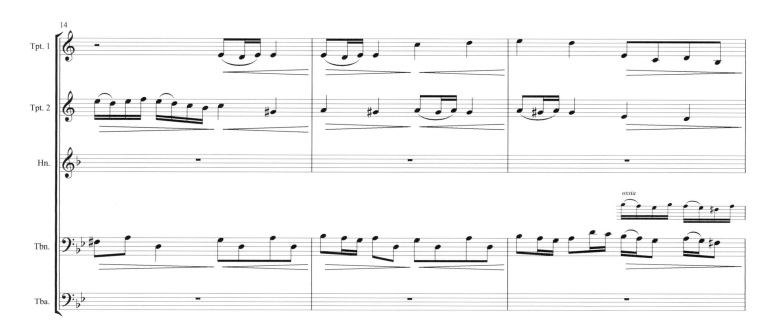

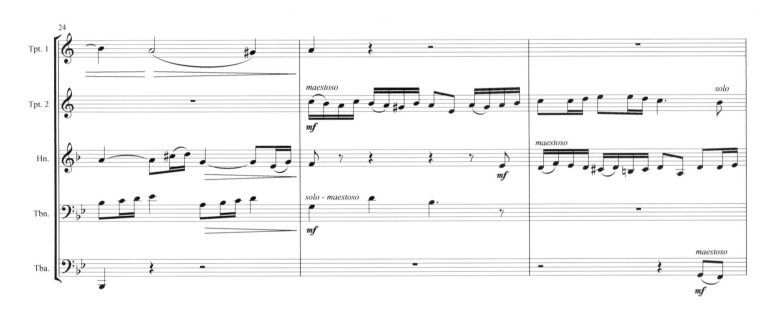

FUGUE IN G MINOR
(The Little)

Johann Sebastian Bach
Arranged by Caleb Hudson

© 2016 Canadian Brass Publications
All Rights Reserved. International Copyright Secured.

Trumpet 2 in B♭

FUGUE IN G MINOR
(The Little)

Johann Sebastian Bach
Arranged by Caleb Hudson

© 2016 Canadian Brass Publications
All Rights Reserved.   International Copyright Secured.

Horn in F

FUGUE IN G MINOR
(The Little)

Johann Sebastian Bach
Arranged by Caleb Hudson

© 2016 Canadian Brass Publications
All Rights Reserved. International Copyright Secured.

FUGUE IN G MINOR
(The Little)

Johann Sebastian Bach
Arranged by Caleb Hudson

© 2016 Canadian Brass Publications
All Rights Reserved.   International Copyright Secured.

Tuba

FUGUE IN G MINOR
(The Little)

Johann Sebastian Bach
Arranged by Caleb Hudson

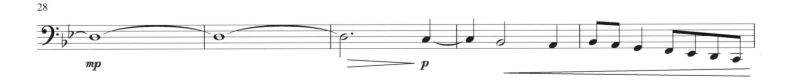

© 2016 Canadian Brass Publications
All Rights Reserved. International Copyright Secured.

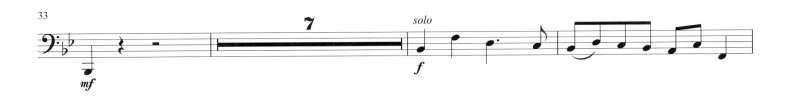

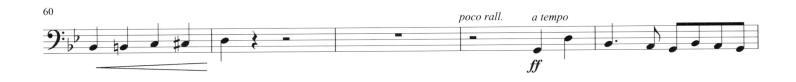

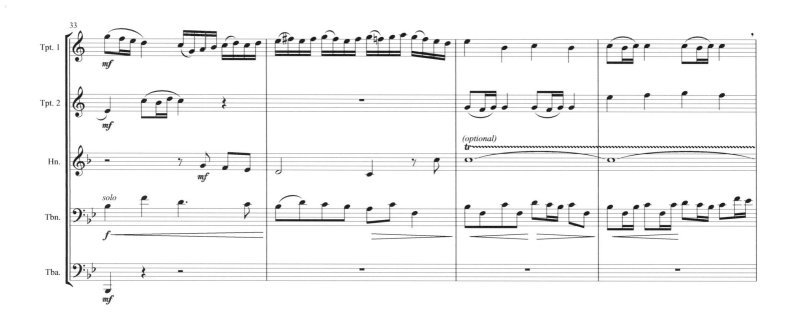

5

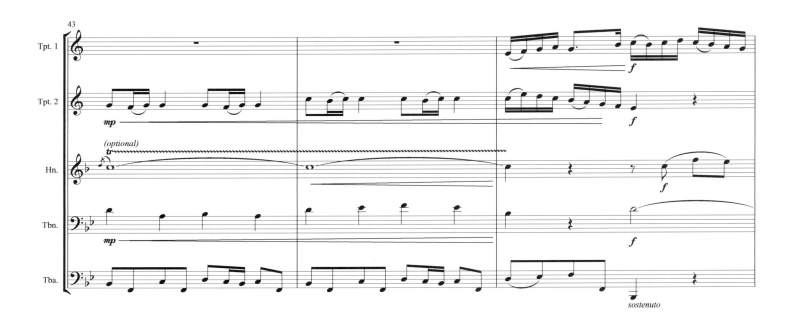

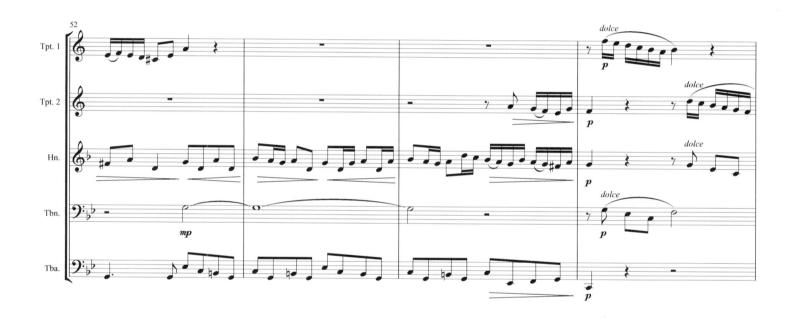

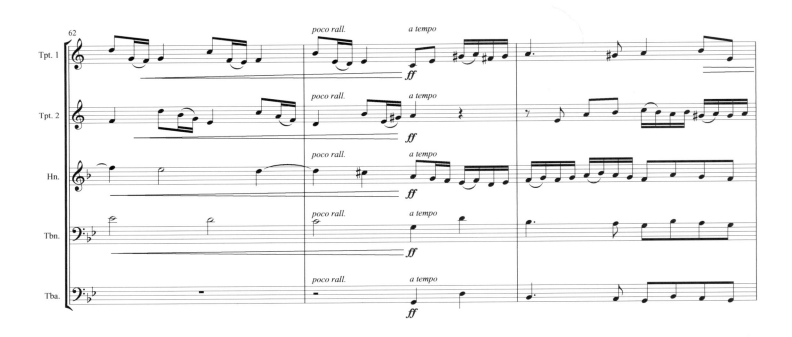